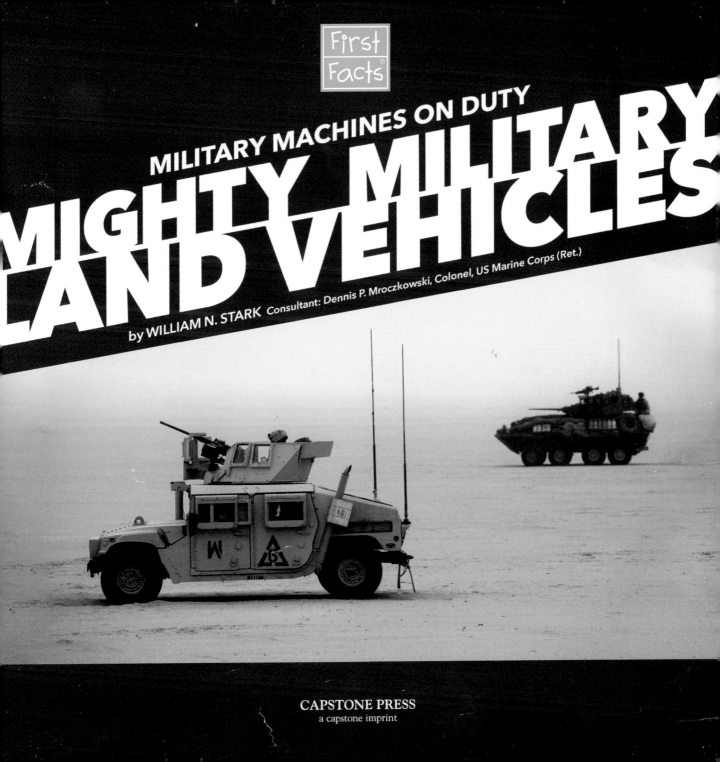

First Facts®

MILITARY MACHINES ON DUTY

MIGHTY MILITARY LAND VEHICLES

by WILLIAM N. STARK Consultant: Dennis P. Mroczkowski, Colonel, US Marine Corps (Ret.)

CAPSTONE PRESS
a capstone imprint

First Facts are published by Capstone Press,
1710 Roe Crest Drive, North Mankato, Minnesota 56003
www.mycapstone.com

Library of Congress Cataloging-in-Publication Data
Stark, William N.
  Mighty military land vehicles / by William N. Stark.
    pages cm. – (First facts. Military machines on duty)
  Includes bibliographical references and index.
  Summary: "Gives readers a quick look at modern military land vehicles"– Provided
by publisher.
  Audience: Grades K-3.
  ISBN 978-1-4914-8848-5 (hardcover)
  ISBN 978-1-4914-8852-2 (ebook pdf)
  1. Vehicles, Military–United States–Juvenile literature. I. Title.
  UC343.S75 2016
  355.8'3–dc23   2015029641

Editorial Credits: Mandy Robbins, editor; Kristi Carlson and Katelin Plekkenpol,
designers; Jo Miller, media researcher; Gene Bentdahl, production specialist

Photo Credits: AP Images, 21; U.S. Army photo by Sgt. Antonieta Rico, 11; U.S.
Marine Corps photo by Cpl Stephen M Kwietniak, 5, Cpl. Ali Azimi, Cover (top),
17, Cpl. Timothy R. Childers, 1, Lance Cpl. Andrew M. Blanco, III MEF Combat
Camera, 13; U.S. Navy photo by MC2 Michael Lindsey, 19, PH1 Arlo Abrahamson,
9; US Army National Guard photo by Sgt. 1st Class William Gates, 15; Wikimedia/
AlfvanBeem, Cover (bottom), 7

Design Element: Shutterstock: Grebnev (metal texture background)

Printed in the United States of America in North Mankato, Minnesota.
092015   009221CGS16

TABLE OF CONTENTS

TOP TECH FOR TOUGH JOBS

Military vehicles have the best modern technology. They deliver food, medicine, and other supplies. These tough machines also carry soldiers, nurses, and doctors. They bound over rough **terrain** and cruise at top speeds. Military vehicles combine power and protection to keep people safe.

terrain—the surface of the land

M60A1

A rumbling tank leads a line of trucks carrying soldiers. Oh no! A wide gap in the land appears. The **convoy** stops. Luckily, this tank carries a 60-foot (18.3-meter) bridge. When needed, the bridge expands across rifts, rivers, or valleys. All the soldiers and materials safely cross the gap. The bridge folds up on top of the tank.

FACT:

The M60A1 Armored Vehicle Launch Bridge weighs 56.6 tons (51 metric tons) and is 31 feet (9.4 m) long.

convoy—soldiers traveling together in military vehicles for protection

SCORPION DESERT PATROL VEHICLE

The Scorpion Desert Patrol Vehicle (DPV) carries up to three U.S. Navy Seals. It can travel on regular roads or **veer** off into rough, uneven terrain. The DPV quickly delivers people into dangerous areas. Those people gather intelligence for the United States. They can also call in **air strikes** or perform other special missions.

veer–to change direction or turn suddenly

air strike–an attack from armed aircraft on a target

M1117 GUARDIAN

The M1117 Guardian weighs
15 tons (13.6 metric tons). But
it's light compared to other
armored vehicles. The Guardian's
crew can see in all directions from
the inside. This machine detects
dangerous chemical weapon attacks.
It protected soldiers in Iraq from
roadside mines and other explosives.

armored vehicle–an automobile or craft with a protective metal covering

AMPHIBIOUS ASSAULT VEHICLE (AAV7)

This **amphibious** machine can travel through water and on land. The AAV7 launches from a naval ship into the ocean. It moves over the ocean's surface and then up onto sandy beaches. It holds up to 25 Marines. The Marines have nicknamed the AAV7 "amtrac," short for "amphibious tractor."

amphibious—a vehicle or craft that can travel over land and also over or in water

HMMWV

The HMMWV is usually called the Humvee. The military designed it to replace the military jeep. This lightly armored vehicle has power delivered to all four wheels. It can serve as an ambulance or carry weapons. The Humvee moves up to four soldiers and their supplies through difficult terrain.

FACT:

"HMMWV" stands for High Mobility Multipurpose Wheeled Vehicle.

M1 ABRAMS TANK

The M1 Abrams tank has served the U.S. military since 1980. It is 32 feet (9.8 m) long and 12 feet (3.7 m) wide. The M1A1 can reach 45 miles (72 kilometers) per hour. Four people can operate the tank in any weather on nearly any terrain. The M1 tank often leads infantry units for protection.

BUFFALO H MRAP VEHICLE

Mine Resistant Ambush Protected (MRAP) vehicles can withstand a dangerous threat to Marines—the **IED**. The vehicle's underside is built to hold up after an explosion. Soldiers inside the vehicle can operate a long robotic arm. The arm can inspect suspicious objects in the road or disable IEDs.

IED—stands for Improvised Explosive Device; IEDs are homemade bombs often made with material not usually found in bombs

AMAZING BUT TRUE!

Women have come a long way in the U.S. military. In the past they did not take part in active combat. But in 1989 Army Captain Linda Bray became the first woman to do so. She and her soldiers came upon enemy troops in Panama. Captain Bray commanded an army jeep to drive through a fence. Her soldiers took enemy weapons and a prisoner. As of 2013 the U.S. Army allowed women in combat.

GLOSSARY

air strike *(AYR STRYKE)*—an attack from armed aircraft on a target

amphibious *(am-FI-bee-uhs)*—a vehicle or craft that can travel over land and also over or in water

armored vehicle *(AR-muhrd VEE-uh-kuhl)*—an automobile or craft with a protective metal covering

convoy *(KAHN-voy)*—soldiers traveling together in military vehicles for protection

IED *(EYE-ee-dee)*—stands for Improvised Explosive Device; IEDs are homemade bombs often made with material not usually found in bombs

infantry *(IN-fuhn-tree)*—soldiers trained to fight on foot

terrain *(tuh-RAYN)*—the surface of the land

veer *(VEER)*—to change direction or turn suddenly

READ MORE

Bell, Samantha S. *Powerful Military Vehicles*. Ready for Military Action. Minneapolis: Core Library, an imprint of Abdo Publishing, 2015.

Clay, Kathryn. *My First Guide to Military Vehicles*. My First Guides. North Mankato, Minn.: Capstone Press, 2015.

Wesley, Jack. *Military Vehicles*. Scholastic Discover More Readers. New York: Scholastic Paperback Nonfiction, 2014.

INTERNET SITES

FactHound offers a safe, fun way to find Internet sites related to this book. All of the sites on FactHound have been researched by our staff.

Here's all you do:

Visit *www.facthound.com*

Type in this code: 9781491488485

Super-cool stuff!

Check out projects, games and lots more at
www.capstonekids.com

CRITICAL THINKING USING THE COMMON CORE

1. What advantages do you think the M117 Guardian might have in battle compared to the M1 Abrams tank? (Key Ideas and Details)

2. Why do you think the United States military kept women out of combat roles in the past?(Integration of Knowledge and Ideas)

INDEX